Prayer to Saint Nicholas

Saint Nicholas, faithful disciple of Jesus Christ, pray for us.

Saint Nicholas, example of Christian love, pray for us.

Saint Nicholas, helper of the poor and needy, pray for us.

Saint Nicholas, champion of orphans and widows, pray for us.

Saint Nicholas, protector of those who sail at sea, pray for us.

Saint Nicholas, defender of the true faith, pray for us.

Saint Nicholas, patron of children around the world, pray for us.

Saint Nicholas, secret giver of gifts, pray for us.

Saint Nicholas, the great wonderworker, pray for us.

Saint Nicholas, our friend in Heaven, pray for us.

Amen.

I dedicate this story to
my granddaughter, Chloe Sophia,
and all children everywhere,
with the hope that they too
may discover the real secret about Santa.

—*Cornelia Mary Bilinsky*

∽∾

For my husband Ken, with love.

—*Candace Camling*

SANTA'S
Secret Story

Written by Cornelia Mary Bilinsky

Illustrated by Candace Camling

Pauline
BOOKS & MEDIA
Boston

Library of Congress Cataloging-in-Publication Data

Bilinsky, Cornelia Mary.

Santa's secret story / written by Cornelia Mary Bilinsky ; illustrated by Candace Camling.

p. cm.

ISBN 0-8198-7160-5

1. Santa Claus. 2. Nicholas, Saint, Bp. of Myra. I. Camling, Candace. II. Title.

GT4985.B517 2011

394.2663--dc22

2011011128

Illustrated by Candace Camling
Design by Mary Joseph Peterson, FSP

"P" and PAULINE are registered trademarks of the Daughters of St. Paul.

Copyright © 2011 Cornelia Mary Bilinsky

Published by Pauline Books & Media, 50 Saint Pauls Avenue, Boston, MA 02130-3491

Printed in the U.S.A.

SSS VSAUSAPEOILL4-110015 7160-5

www.pauline.org

Pauline Books & Media is the publishing house of the Daughters of St. Paul, an international congregation of women religious serving the Church with the communications media.

2 3 4 5 6 7 8 9   18 17 16 15 14

"I know a secret about Santa," said Maya.

"What secret?" asked Rachel, glancing across the street. On the rooftop of a neighbor's house, an inflated Santa was swaying and bobbing in the wind.

"I don't know if I should tell you," said Maya.
"But I'm your friend!"
"Well . . . ," Maya whispered into Rachel's ear,
"Santa lives in heaven!" She waved and ran off home.
Rachel laughed and waved back. Maya always said
the funniest things.

"What's the secret?" asked Zachary, Rachel's little brother.

"Were you listening?" Rachel was annoyed. "It's nothing. Forget it!"

Later at bedtime, Rachel began to worry. *What did Maya mean? Only people who died lived in heaven. Had Santa died? If so, there would be no presents in her stocking and nothing under the tree.*

Rachel couldn't sleep. She lay in her bed, looking at her night light. It was a pretty light, shaped like an angel. Seeing it reminded Rachel to say her Guardian Angel prayer.

Angel of God, guardian mine,
   beside me always stay.
Morning, evening, day and night,
   help me in every way!

"And oh!" Rachel added, "I have a BIG question for you. Does Santa live in heaven?"

"Rachel!" said a voice softly.

Rachel opened her eyes. She heard music, the tinkling sound of a thousand tiny silver bells. Before her stood an angel surrounded by radiant light. A feeling of peace wrapped around Rachel like a warm blanket.

"Are you my guardian angel?" she whispered.

The angel smiled. "I have been sent to help you find the answer to your BIG question."

"Oh," cried Rachel, "can you do that?"

"Let's find out!" said the angel, bending low.

Rachel touched the tips of the angel's wings.

WHOOSH!

Suddenly, they were in a large room, richly furnished with sofas and draperies such as Rachel had never seen before.

"Where are we?" she asked.

"We have gone back in time, seventeen hundred years, to a seaport near a city called Myra."

Rachel looked around. She saw a young man sitting at a table, unrolling a scroll.

"Who is that?" Rachel asked.

"*That* is the man you know as Santa Claus," said the angel.

"It can't be!" Rachel objected. The man was wearing a simple brown robe. A wooden cross hung around his neck.

"Why don't you ask him yourself then?" the angel suggested.

Timidly, Rachel stepped forward.
"Excuse me, sir. Are you Santa Claus?"
The young man looked up. His eyes were kind.
"My name is Nicholas," he said.

"What are you reading?" Rachel asked.

Turning back to his scroll, Nicholas read aloud: "To you is born this day in the city of David a Savior, who is the Messiah, Christ the Lord. This will be a sign for you: you will find a child wrapped in swaddling clothes and lying in a manger."

"It's the Christmas story!" Rachel cried.

"It's the story of God's greatest gift!" said Nicholas. His eyes glistened with tears. "Jesus Christ, the Son of God *chose* to be born in a poor stable. He came to show us how much God loves us. He came to save us! I have an idea about what I can do to show Jesus how grateful I am." He glanced around the room. "This beautiful house belonged to my parents before they died. If I sell it, I can give everything to help the poor."

"*Everything?*" asked Rachel in surprise.

The angel tapped Rachel on the shoulder.
Again Rachel touched the tips of the angel's
glowing wings.

WHOOSH!

They were standing at the window of a lowly hut. Inside, a man was sitting beside the fireplace. He looked sad and worried. Nearby, three young girls huddled together. Tears were streaming down their cheeks.

"Why are they crying?" Rachel asked.

"Their father used to be a rich man, but now he has nothing," explained the angel. "His daughters may have to live as beggars or slaves."

"That's terrible!" Rachel was shocked. "Why doesn't somebody help them?"

There was a sudden noise above the hut. Rachel looked up.

"Oh!" she cried, "It's Santa—I mean, Nicholas! What's he doing on the roof?"

Inside the hut, something fell out of the chimney and landed in a wool stocking that had been hung in front of the fireplace to dry. Puzzled, the man reached into the stocking and pulled out a small burlap bag. When he shook it, shiny gold coins jingled and rolled onto the floor.

The girls came running across the room. "What is it, Papa?"

The man threw himself onto his knees.

"Oh my dear daughters! The Lord has saved us! He has given me these gold coins so that I can provide for you. Thanks be to God!"

Confused, Rachel turned to the angel. "But it was *Nicholas* who did it!"

The angel smiled. "Yes, Nicholas is using his riches to help people who are poor and needy."

"But why didn't he just give the man the money? Why did he throw it down the chimney?"

"Nicholas likes to give his gifts in secret. But why not ask him about that yourself?"

Rachel touched the angel's wings.

WHOOSH!

In an instant they were on a snow-covered rooftop with Nicholas. He motioned to Rachel to sit beside him.

"Why do you give your gifts in secret?" Rachel asked.

"I want people to thank *God*, not me! Remember, the greatest gift is God's love. I am just happy to bring his love to others," explained Nicholas. A beautiful light was shining around them. Just then Rachel remembered her big question.

"Do you live in heaven?" she asked.

Nicholas nodded.

"Then you *did* die!" Rachel pondered for a moment. "But you're still Santa Claus, aren't you? The angel said you were!"

The angel interrupted. "All his life, Nicholas helped people. For many years he was the Bishop of Myra, beloved for his wonderful works. Now he is SAINT Nicholas. He lives in heaven but he keeps on doing wonderful works. He is especially good to children."

The saint's eyes twinkled merrily. "The angel is right, Rachel. And *you* can help me."

"Me?" asked Rachel. "How?"

"By sharing the love of God with others and by doing good. *That's* the secret. You can even give your gifts *in secret,* if you want."

Rachel's eyes gleamed with understanding.

"In secret, hmmmmm. . . ."

"Rachel, wake up! It's morning!"

Zachary was bouncing on Rachel's bed.

"Tonight Santa is coming! We have to hang up our stockings!" He was dangling two Christmas stockings, his own and Rachel's.

Rachel sat up. She reached out to grab her stocking away from Zachary, but she stopped herself. Was she imagining it, or did her angel light flicker? Suddenly she *remembered*.

"Okay, Zachary," Rachel said, "I'll help you hang up the stockings."

Zachary beamed and Rachel's heart grew warm. She was almost certain she heard the tinkling sound of a thousand tiny silver bells.

It felt good, sharing God's love. Maybe later, when Zachary wasn't looking, she would secretly put a little gift for him under the tree, something to make him happy.

"Zachary, remember that secret you asked me about?" Rachel whispered.
"Yes!" he answered with excitement.
Rachel smiled. "Want to hear it?"

*C*ornelia Mary Bilinsky was born and raised in Manitoba. She received her Bachelor of Arts Degree in English and Theology from St. Paul's College at the University of Manitoba. She taught English at the high school level as well as English as a Second Language. Cornelia's husband is a Ukrainian Catholic priest. They have one daughter and one granddaughter. Since 1981, Cornelia has been involved in ministry at Ukrainian Catholic parishes in Ontario where her husband serves. Her most fulfilling work has been the religious education of children for whom she has created many stories, plays, and songs. Cornelia currently resides in Oshawa, Ontario. *Santa's Secret Story* is her first published book.

Candace Camling works as a freelance illustrator from her home studio in Des Moines, Iowa. She earned her Bachelor of Fine Arts Degree in Illustration from Kendall College of Art and Design in 2007, and was proud to graduate as Valedictorian and winner of the Studio Excellence Award. Candace teaches children's classes at the Des Moines Art Center and enjoys working in watercolor, oils, and digital media. She has done art work for American Greetings, Manley Toy Network, and various other clients as far away as Australia. A member of the Society of Children's Book Writers and Illustrators, Candace's main passion is illustrating for children. *Santa's Secret Story* is her first book with Pauline Kids.

Tales and Legends from

The 3 Trees

The Little Lost Lamb

Santa's Secret Story

Coming soon!

The Saint Who Fought the Dragon:
The Story of St. George

Who are the Daughters of St. Paul?

We are Catholic sisters. Our mission is to be like Saint Paul and tell everyone about Jesus! There are so many ways for people to communicate with each other. We want to use all of them so everyone will know how much God loves us. We do this by printing books (you're holding one!), making radio shows, singing, helping people at our bookstores, using the Internet, and in many other ways.

Visit our Web site at www.pauline.org

BOOKS & MEDIA

The Daughters of St. Paul operate book and media centers at the following addresses. Visit, call, or write the one nearest you today, or find us at www.pauline.org

CALIFORNIA
3908 Sepulveda Blvd, Culver City, CA 90230 — 310-397-8676
935 Brewster Avenue, Redwood City, CA 94063 — 650-369-4230
5945 Balboa Avenue, San Diego, CA 92111 — 858-565-9181

FLORIDA
145 S.W. 107th Avenue, Miami, FL 33174 — 305-559-6715

HAWAII
1143 Bishop Street, Honolulu, HI 96813 — 808-521-2731

ILLINOIS
172 North Michigan Avenue, Chicago, IL 60601 — 312-346-4228

LOUISIANA
4403 Veterans Memorial Blvd, Metairie, LA 70006 — 504-887-7631

MASSACHUSETTS
885 Providence Hwy, Dedham, MA 02026 — 781-326-5385

MISSOURI
9804 Watson Road, St. Louis, MO 63126 — 314-965-3512

NEW YORK
64 West 38th Street, New York, NY 10018 — 212-754-1110

SOUTH CAROLINA
243 King Street, Charleston, SC 29401 — 843-577-0175

VIRGINIA
1025 King Street, Alexandria, VA 22314 — 703-549-3806

CANADA
3022 Dufferin Street, Toronto, ON M6B 3T5 — 416-781-9131

Biography of Saint Nicholas

Long before anyone ever heard the name Santa Claus, there lived a man named Nicholas. He was born in the year A.D. 270 to a wealthy Christian family in Patara, a Mediterranean seaport in Lycia (presently in Turkey). As a young boy, Nicholas heard the call of Jesus to follow in his footsteps. When his parents died, he sold his worldly goods and used the money to help the poor and needy.

Nicholas became a monk and later was ordained to the priesthood. In 313, he was elected Bishop of the city of Myra, the capital of Lycia. Before long, he was well known and greatly loved for his kindness and compassion, especially toward children and those in grave trouble, on land or at sea. In 325, when the bishops of the Christian world met in Nicea for the first ecumenical council, Nicholas was among them. He strongly defended the true faith against those who were attacking it with false ideas.

Nicholas died in the year 343, and afterward many miracles were attributed to his prayers on behalf of seafarers, children, and families in distress. Stories about his wonderful works spread throughout the Christian world. He quickly became a favorite saint, often called Nicholas the Giftgiver or the Great Wonderworker. His feast day is December 6 (or December 19 for those churches that follow the Julian calendar).